BOOKWORMS

Animal Structures

Hair, Fur, and Spines

Derek Miller

Cavendish Square
New York

Published in 2019 by Cavendish Square Publishing, LLC
243 5th Avenue, Suite 136, New York, NY 10016

First Edition

Website: cavendishsq.com

Library of Congress Cataloging-in-Publication Data

Names: Miller, Derek, author.
Title: Hair, fur, and spines / Derek Miller.
Description: First edition. | New York : Cavendish Square, 2019. | Series: Animal structures | Audience: Grades K-3. | Includes index.
Identifiers: LCCN 2018017152 (print) | LCCN 2018019576 (ebook) | ISBN 9781502641953 (ebook) |
ISBN 9781502641946 (library bound) | ISBN 9781502641922 (paperback) | ISBN 9781502641939 (6 pack)
Subjects: LCSH: Hair--Juvenile literature. | Fur--Juvenile literature. | Spine--Juvenile literature. | Spines (Zoology)--Juvenile literature.
Classification: LCC QL942 (ebook) | LCC QL942 .M49 2019 (print) | DDC 599.147--dc23
LC record available at https://lccn.loc.gov/2018017152

Editorial Director: David McNamara
Copy Editor: Nathan Heidelberger
Associate Art Director: Alan Sliwinski
Designer: Megan Metté
Production Coordinator: Karol Szymczuk
Photo Research: J8 Media

The photographs in this book are used by permission and through the courtesy of: Cover (left to right) 1tomm/Shutterstock.com, Phugunfire/Shutterstock.com, Luca Nichetti/Shutterstock.com; p. 5 Bigandt.com/Shutterstock.com; p. 7 Vaclav Sebek/Shutterstock.com; p. 9 Sergey Gorshkov/ Minden Pictures/Getty Images; p. 11 Chavarin Jantanabuppa/Shutterstock.com; p. 13 David Trood /Stone/Getty Images; p. 15 Serge Vero/iStock.com; p. 17 Sainam51/Shutterstock.com; p. 19 Damocean/iStock.com; p. 21 Olya Solodenko/iStock.com.

Printed in the United States of America

Contents

People are **mammals**.

Dogs are mammals.

Mammals have **fur** or **hair**.

Fur keeps animals warm.

It traps body heat.

Some mammals have a lot of fur.

They live in the cold.

They need thick fur to stay warm.

Some mammals have hair.

They don’t need fur to
stay warm.

Humans have hair.

It doesn't keep them very warm.

Humans use clothes to stay warm.

Hairs can be many colors.

Hair and fur can help animals hide.

Some animals have **spines**.

Spines are sharp.

Spines cover their bodies.

Spines keep animals safe.

They poke other animals.

Spines make other animals stay away.

Fur and hair keep
animals warm.

Spines keep them safe.

New Words

fur (FUHR) The coat of an animal.

hair (HEHR) Something that grows to help keep a person warm.

mammals (MAHM-muhls) Animals that have fur or hair.

spines (SPYNS) The sharp hairs that keep some animals safe.

Index

About the Author

Derek Miller is a teacher and writer. He is the author of many books for young students. He likes to write about animals.

About BOOKWORMS

Bookworms help independent readers gain reading confidence through high-frequency words, simple sentences, and strong picture/text support. Each book explores a concept that helps children relate what they read to the world they live in.